Forecasting the Weather

by Donna Latham

PEARSON
Scott Foresman

Editorial Offices: Glenview, Illinois • Parsippany, New Jersey • New York, New York
Sales Offices: Needham, Massachusetts • Duluth, Georgia • Glenview, Illinois
Coppell, Texas • Ontario, California • Mesa, Arizona

Every effort has been made to secure permission and provide appropriate credit for photographic material. The publisher deeply regrets any omission and pledges to correct errors called to its attention in subsequent editions.

Unless otherwise acknowledged, all photographs are the property of Scott Foresman, a division of Pearson Education.

Photo locators denoted as follows: Top (T), Center (C), Bottom (B), Left (L), Right (R), Background (Bkgd)

Opener: Corbis; 3 Corbis; 4 (BL) Corbis, (BR) ©Dorling Kindersley; 5 ©Dorling Kindersley; 6 ©Dorling Kindersley; 8 ©Dorling Kindersley; 9 ©Dorling Kindersley; 10 PhotoEdit; 11 Corbis; 12 ©argus/Peter Arnold, Inc.; 13 Stephen Oliver/©Dorling Kindersley; 14 Brand X Pictures; 17 (T) Steve Gorton/©Dorling Kindersley, (B) Corbis; 18 ©Dorling Kindersley; 19 ©Dorling Kindersley; 20 ©Dorling Kindersley; 22 Corbis

ISBN: 0-328-13507-0

Copyright © Pearson Education, Inc.

All Rights Reserved. Printed in the United States of America. This publication is protected by Copyright, and permission should be obtained from the publisher prior to any prohibited reproduction, storage in a retrieval system, or transmission in any form by any means, electronic, mechanical, photocopying, recording, or likewise. For information regarding permission(s), write to: Permissions Department, Scott Foresman, 1900 East Lake Avenue, Glenview, Illinois 60025.

3 4 5 6 7 8 9 10 V0G1 14 13 12 11 10 09 08 07 06

Today's Weather

How would you describe the weather today in your town or city? Is it humid, windy, or cold? Maybe it's dry, or perhaps it's rainy or foggy.

You probably thought about the weather when you got dressed this morning. Perhaps you bundled up in extra layers of clothing because it was chilly out. Or maybe you're wearing lighter clothes because the weather is warm. You might even be dressed in several layers of clothing.

As you read this, is the weather where you live the same as it was when you awoke? Or has it changed completely? Chances are, depending on the region in which you live, that the weather will shift throughout the day, which is why dressing in layers can be so useful.

Weather affects every part of our lives. It can affect what we wear, what we eat, what we do, and even how we feel. Our weather can be as gentle as a light rain or as harsh as a blizzard. Either way, weather is impossible to avoid, so it's a constant part of our lives.

Every day we look at **weather forecasts,** or predictions about what kind of weather to expect. Weather forecasts affect the jobs of many people, from airline pilots to truck drivers to fishermen. Even families rely on weather forecasts.

Suppose it has been raining for several days where the Garcia family lives. How is the rain affecting their lives? Josh Garcia's baseball games have been rained out three times in a row. Mrs. Garcia has wanted to plant her outdoor vegetable garden, but the soggy ground won't let her.

After visiting an online weather source, the Garcias found the ten-day forecast shown below. Now they'll know which day should have the best weather for playing baseball and planting a garden!

Weather forecasts are important, but how are they made? Weather tools are used to gather information about weather conditions such as wind, pressure, temperature, humidity, and precipitation.

Using this weather forecast, the Garcias can see that Wednesday should be the best day for outdoor activities!

10-Day Forecast

Day	Conditions	High/Low	Precipitation %
Tonight	T-storms late	49°	60%
Tues.	Isolated T-storms	67° / 52°	30%
Wed.	Partly Cloudy	67° / 51°	10%
Thurs.	Isolated T-storms	73° / 50°	30%
Fri.	Mostly Cloudy	71° / 54°	20%
Sat.	Scattered T-storms	72° / 55°	40%
Sun.	Scattered T-storms	78° / 60°	40%
Mon.	Few Showers	74° / 55°	30%
Tues.	Light Rain	72° / 51°	60%
Wed.	Scattered Showers	73° / 53°	40%

Source: The Weather Channel

The data collected by the weather tools can be compiled to create a weather forecast. But even with these tools, we need to understand a few basic facts about the causes of weather before we attempt to create a weather forecast.

First of all, without the Sun, we would not have weather. Second, the air surrounding Earth is made up of different gases. Third, the heat generated by the Sun warms the air and sets it in motion. Whether it is sinking, rising, or shifting sideways, the air is always moving.

How does this movement affect us? It creates pressure systems, and changes in air pressure are especially important to weather forecasts. When the pressure falls, this indicates a storm is on the way. But when the pressure rises, this signals that fair weather will continue or arrive soon. Combining this knowledge with data from weather tools leads to accurate weather forecasts.

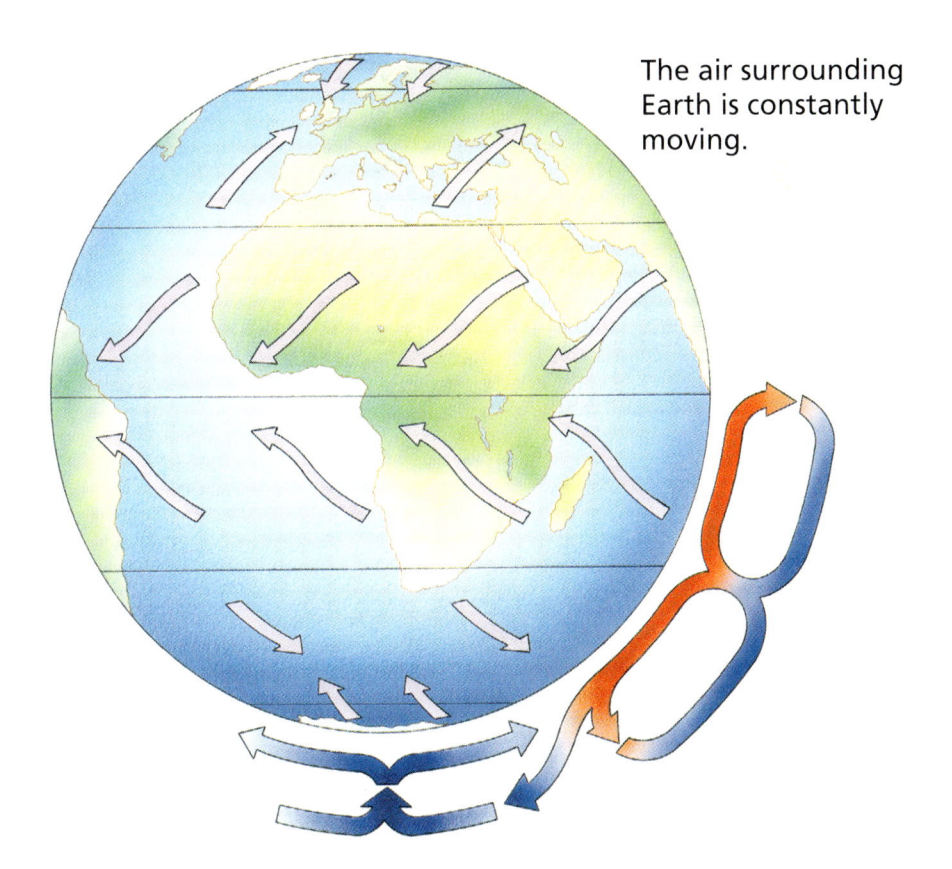

The air surrounding Earth is constantly moving.

5

Layers of the Atmosphere

The **atmosphere** is the huge bubble of air, formed of different gases, that surrounds Earth. Scientists divide the atmosphere into five layers—the troposphere, the stratosphere, the mesosphere, the thermosphere, and the exosphere.

The lowest layer, which extends upward from Earth's surface for seven miles, is called the **troposphere.** Clouds form in the troposphere because it is the densest part of the atmosphere. We inhabit the troposphere because its air gives us the oxygen we need in order to live. And weather happens in the troposphere!

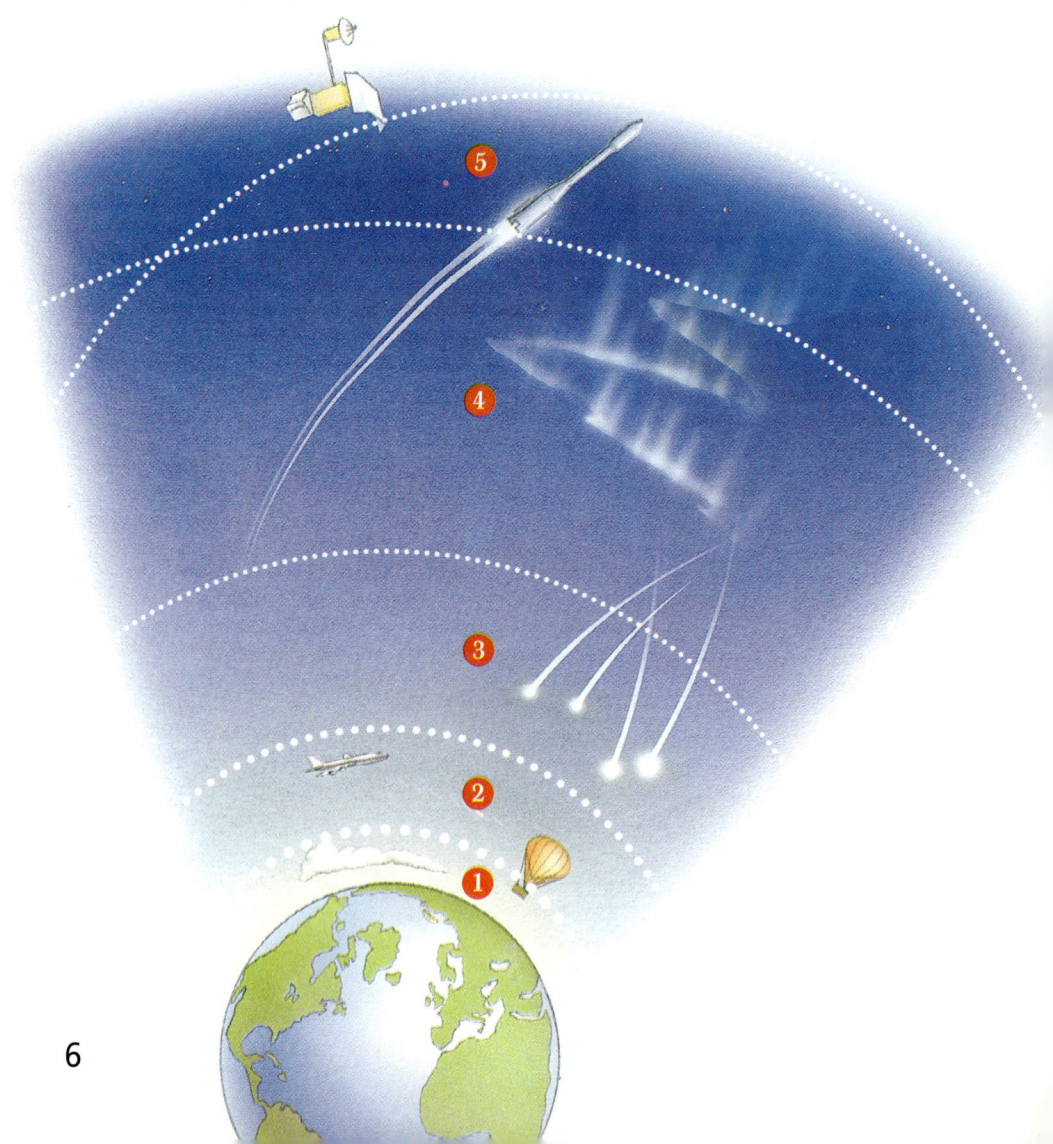

1. Troposphere
Stretching from the ground to about seven miles upward, the troposphere is where weather occurs. That's because this layer holds the most water vapor. The troposphere is the densest layer of the atmosphere and the only one to interact with Earth's surface. Temperatures at the top of the troposphere are lower than those at the bottom.

2. Stratosphere
Here, seven to thirty miles above the ground, the air is calm and clear. This is why airplanes soar into the stratosphere for a smooth flight! You have probably heard of the ozone layer. The stratosphere is where it's located, about fifteen miles above Earth.

3. Mesosphere
Temperatures drop steadily in this layer. From thirty to fifty miles above Earth, this is the coldest place in the entire atmosphere. Temperatures can fall to -130°F (-90°C) here!

4. Thermosphere
The thermosphere brings a huge jump in temperature. From 50 to 435 miles above Earth, the thermosphere is the hottest place in the whole atmosphere. Temperatures can actually climb to 2,690°F (1,475°C) in the thermosphere! The aurora borealis, the colored light visible at northern latitudes, happens here.

5. Exosphere
The place where satellites orbit Earth, the exosphere is the outermost part of the atmosphere. At 435 to 500 miles from the ground, it is made up of the gases oxygen, helium, nitrogen, and argon.

Meteorology . . . Then

Meteorology is the science of studying and forecasting the weather. Scientists who observe and predict the weather are called **meteorologists.** Did you know that people have been fascinated by the weather for thousands of years? Many have observed it and tried to make sense of it.

Meteorology was practiced in many early cultures, where exciting myths were told to explain weather events. If you read ancient mythology, you will see that some of it deals extensively with weather.

For instance, the Aztecs worshipped a Sun god named Tonatiuh. They believed that Tonatiuh was born every day at sunrise and died every evening at sunset, and they made offerings so the Sun would return. Native Americans believed in a powerful spirit called the Thunderbird. Stories described lightning flashing from the bird's beak and thunder coming from the flapping of the bird's wings.

The ancient Greek philosopher Aristotle wrote a book to describe weather phenomena, or unusual events. The title of his work, *Meteorologica,* gave us today's term *meteorology.*

George Washington, Thomas Jefferson, and Ben Franklin all enjoyed weather watching. Washington and Jefferson kept daily weather logs. Known for his experiments with lightning, Franklin also wrote *Poor Richard's Almanack*. Printed each year, it contained weather forecasts.

In Native American mythology, the Thunderbird was responsible for thunder and lightning.

The Sun god Tonatiuh is pictured at the center of the ancient Aztec calendar.

Meteorology . . . Now

Have you ever been watching TV and had the program interrupted by a National Weather Service alert? The alerts sound something like this: "We interrupt your regularly scheduled program for the following announcement from the National Weather Service."

Often, a meteorologist like the one below will add to the alert by giving a forecast, such as: "A tornado warning is in effect for Stratford County until 7:45 P.M. This is a Doppler-indicated storm, meaning its wind speed has been measured. If you are in the path of this storm or you see a funnel cloud, take cover. We repeat..."

Local TV stations issue storm watches when their data indicate that the weather conditions are right for a storm to occur. If a storm has actually developed, they will issue a warning and interrupt TV programs. It is important to pay attention to any weather alerts so that you can learn what safety steps you need to follow.

It may seem like TV meteorologists are the only people who study weather. After all, they're the only ones you see on TV talking about it. But behind the scenes, there are many others who forecast and study the weather. These unnoticed weather watchers are always hard at work!

Meteorologists study heat, temperature, and humidity. They measure rain and snow and gather information about the atmosphere by collecting and measuring the gases in the air. Remember the ten-day forecast the Garcia family found? Meteorologists use the data they find to make forecasts like those.

When a twister like this one forms, a weather warning is issued.

Tools of the Trade

Forecasting the weather is really quite tricky because no one really knows what the weather will do. There isn't a one-size-fits-all method of collecting data that meteorologists can use to make accurate forecasts. So, at weather stations like the one shown below, meteorologists collect different kinds of data using many types of instruments. The data provided by these tools is what meteorologists use to make their forecasts. Have you ever seen an instrument that measures weather in some way?

There are about 10,000 fixed, land-based weather stations around the world.

Anemometer

There's a good chance that you have seen a thermometer hanging somewhere. Meteorologists use thermometers to measure the air's temperature and find masses of cold and warm air that can affect pressure systems.

Used to measure wind speed, an **anemometer** allows meteorologists to see in which direction and how quickly the air is moving. Three or four spinning cups are attached at the top of an anemometer. Unless the wind speed is zero, the cups spin. As the wind speed increases, the cups spin faster and faster.

Have you ever seen a weather vane on top of a building? A weather vane shows the wind's direction. The arrow of a weather vane indicates the direction from which the wind is blowing. Winds blow from high-pressure areas to those with low pressure.

A **hygrometer** measures the amount of humidity, or water vapor, in the air. Water vapor makes the air feel damp and makes up clouds, fog, rain, and snow.

Do you have a **barometer** in your home? It's used to measure air pressure. Remember the importance of air pressure? When it changes, the weather does too. Most times when the weather is cloudy, the pressure is low. And most times when the weather is clear, the pressure is high.

Observations on Land

You have learned about how huge Earth's atmosphere is. It's so enormous that no one single country can monitor it, so many countries around the world created the World Meteorological Organization (WMO) in 1951.

Members of the WMO have the responsibility of measuring and reporting atmospheric conditions. They then share the information that they have collected with other members to aid in forecasting future conditions.

New weather forms every second, so conditions must be observed constantly. Weather observations take place on land, in air, and at sea, often using tools more advanced and high tech than thermometers, weather vanes, or barometers.

One such high-tech tool is Doppler radar. **Doppler radar** tracks the air's movement by sending out sound waves and measuring the frequency at which they return. These measurements help meteorologists to warn us in advance of bad weather. For example, Doppler radar helps meteorologists see a tornado forming. Remember how the TV meteorologist's forecast on page 10 included the phrase "Doppler-indicated"? All that meant was that the tornado had been spotted using Doppler radar.

There are more than 150 Doppler radar stations across the United States. They constantly track the wind, moisture, and temperatures of the upper atmosphere.

The Doppler radar shown below can provide us with images of dangerous weather. Using those images, meteorologists can provide up-to-the-minute information about storms and issue watches and warnings when needed.

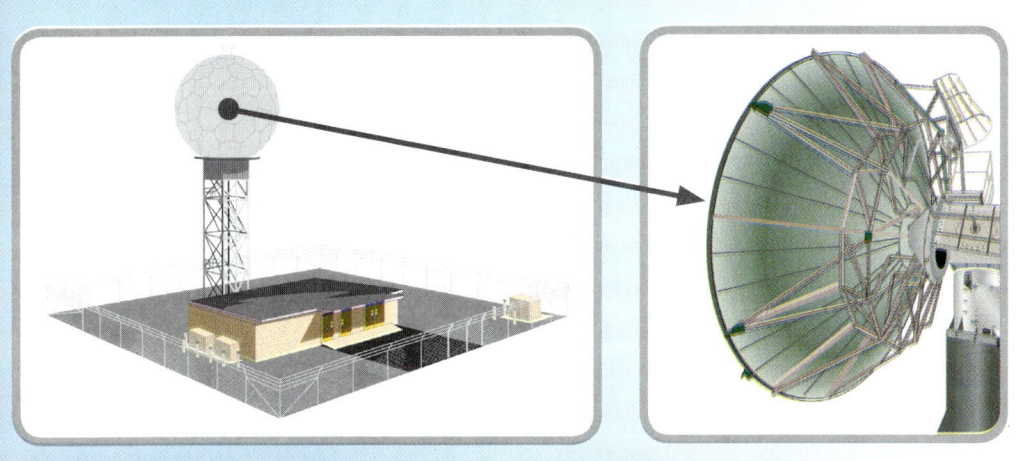

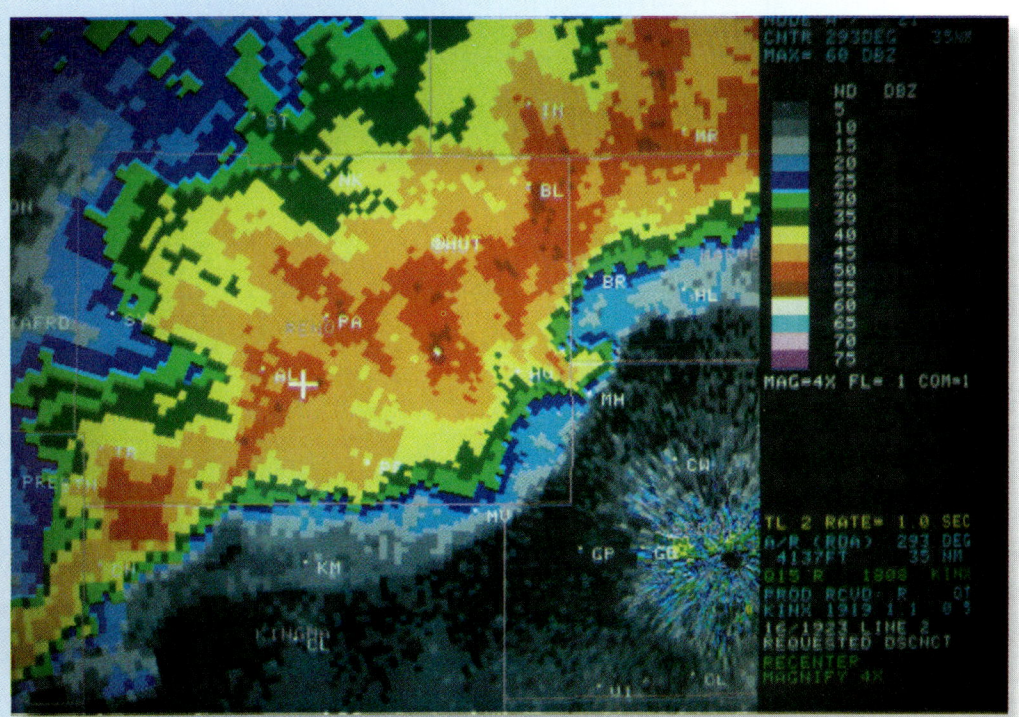

15

Observations from the Air

Like Doppler radar, satellites offer images of dangerous weather. They orbit hundreds of miles above Earth and take pictures of weather patterns, such as hurricanes.

Hurricanes are huge ocean storms. They form when groups of thunderstorms encounter the right atmospheric conditions. Hurricane Andrew formed during August of 1992, striking the Bahamas and the southeastern United States between August 16 and August 28.

The weather map to the right shows three time-lapse photographs, all taken by satellite, of Hurricane Andrew. Hurricane Andrew started off Africa's west coast as a tropical storm, but it became one of the most powerful hurricanes in United States history. Once it moved over land permanently, it lost power and died out.

Meteorologists release hundreds of strong helium balloons containing objects called **radiosondes** twice each day, all around the world. As the balloons soar up to a height 100,000 feet or more in the atmosphere, each radiosonde measures temperature, air pressure, and humidity.

The name "radiosonde" provides you with a clue as to how it works. A radiosonde transmits its data back to land stations until the balloon carrying it bursts. Once this happens, a small parachute opens and carries the radiosonde back to Earth. If it is found, it will be fixed and reused.

The Path of Hurricane Andrew

1. Hurricane Andrew bearing down on Cuba
2. Hurricane Andrew just after it struck southern Florida and the Gulf of Mexico
3. Hurricane Andrew after it passed over the coast of Louisiana

Look at the airplane shown below, and notice how long its nose is. It's extra long in order to hold special instruments used to measure temperature and humidity. If the instruments were anywhere but on the tip of the nose, the data that they recorded would be affected by metals found inside the plane.

Pilots for the National Oceanic and Atmospheric Administration (NOAA) fly special planes like this one in order to observe the weather. Some of NOAA's planes are designed to fly right into the eye of a hurricane!

These special planes are also designed to drop something called a dropwindsonde over the ocean. A dropwindsonde is a kind of radiosonde. It measures air pressure, humidity, and temperature. While the dropwindsonde falls through the sky attached to its parachute, it radios data back to the plane.

Planes are weather watchers in the sky.

Observations at Sea

Like airplanes, ships can be used to record data and observe weather. However, ships can do more than just report on weather conditions. They can also launch weather balloons and place special weather buoys in the water.

While riding the ocean currents, buoys take weather measurements. They send readings to satellites, which send them along to weather stations on land so that scientists can use them to predict the weather.

Some of these buoys are anchored to the ocean floor, while others float freely. In addition to air pressure, wind direction, wind speed, and temperature, some buoys are equipped to measure wave height, strength, and direction. This information is especially helpful in detecting dangerous conditions for ships at sea.

This buoy records weather data.

Weather Maps

You have probably used world maps, state maps, and even road maps before. But have you ever used a weather map? The National Weather Service, which is part of NOAA, updates its weather maps every three hours!

The weather map on the top of page 21 shows the United States, and the color-coded bar at the top indicates temperatures. You can match the colors to the states, which are outlined, to find their temperatures. This map shows that at the time it was created, Texas was experiencing some of the hottest temperatures, while Montana was enduring some of the coolest. Weather maps such as this one are updated nearly every hour because of changing weather.

The map at the bottom of the page is different. Taken from NOAA's Prediction Center, this map displays the predicted weather for the entire country! It shows the general kind of weather that is being forecast.

Now you know what goes into making detailed local forecasts. You have read about the different ways that meteorologists study, record, and predict the weather using many different tools and lots of data.

Weather is always changing, which makes meteorologists' jobs difficult. The good thing is that weather is always happening, giving meteorologists plenty of chances to improve their forecasting skills!

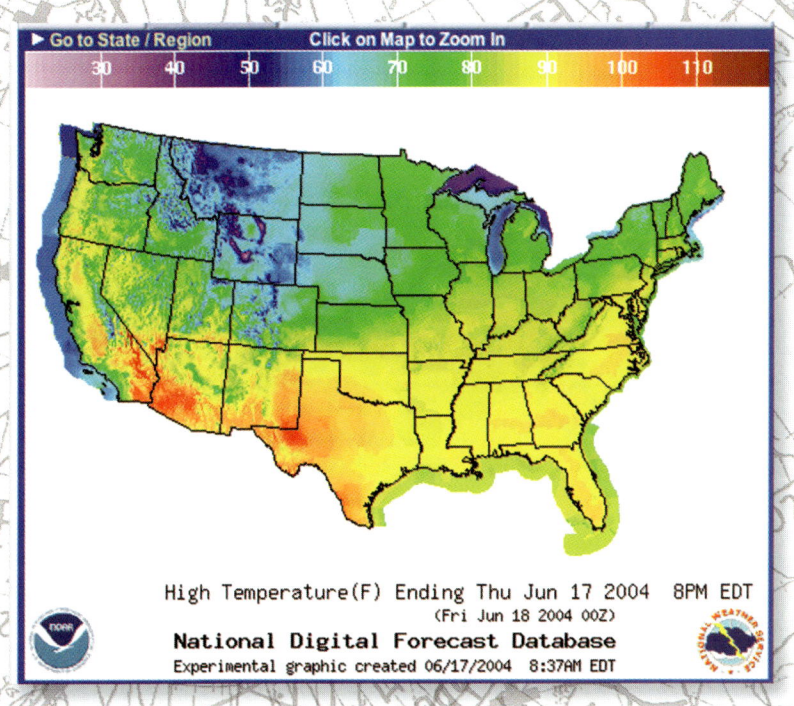

Temperature forecast map

Weather forecast map

21

Now Try This

Weather Forecast

Now that you know how meteorologists study and forecast the weather, you can create your own weather forecast. Using today's technology, you can create a forecast for your town, state, or region. If you wanted to, you could create a forecast for the entire United States, or even some other country or continent!

Up-to-the-minute weather information is available online.

Here's How To Do It!

- The first thing you need to do is collect data about the weather. Use sources such as newspapers, radio and TV reports, and Web sites to study current weather and predicted changes. Find the day's predicted high and low temperatures. Find out the wind speed and direction, as well as the air pressure and humidity.
- If you decide to create a local forecast, try to include what you can observe with your own senses. Can you hear the rumbling of thunder, see bright sunshine, or feel humid air? All are important details that help add depth to a forecast.
- Next, choose how you will show your forecast. You have seen examples of ten-day forecasts, satellite images, and weather maps in this book. Each gives a different way of viewing weather information.
- Now you're ready to write a weather forecast! Be certain to include the specific data you collected about temperature, wind, air pressure, and humidity. With a partner, practice reading your forecast aloud. If possible, present your forecast to your class or family!

Glossary

anemometer *n.* a device for measuring the speed of wind.

atmosphere *n.* air that surrounds Earth.

barometer *n.* a device for measuring air pressure.

Doppler radar *n.* a method of tracking the movement of weather systems.

hygrometer *n.* a device for measuring humidity.

meteorologists *n.* scientists who study and predict the weather.

radiosondes *n.* devices carried into the atmosphere by balloons that use radio to gather and send data.

troposphere *n.* the lowest, most dense layer of atmosphere.

weather forecasts *n.* predictions about weather in the near future.